W9-BCC-923

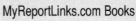
PRESIDENTS

ABRAHAM LINCOLN

A MyReportLinks.com Book

Judy Alter

 MyReportLinks.com Books

an imprint of

Enslow Publishers, Inc.

Box 398, 40 Industrial Road
Berkeley Heights, NJ 07922
USA

For Maddie.

MyReportLinks.com Books, an imprint of Enslow Publishers, Inc.

Library of Congress Cataloging-in-Publication Data

Alter, Judy, 1938–
        Abraham Lincoln : A MyReportLinks.com Book / Judy Alter.
            p. cm. — (Presidents)
        Includes bibliographical references and index.
        Summary: A biography of the president responsible for the Emancipation
Proclamation, Gettysburg Address, and more. Includes Internet links to Web sites,
source documents, and photographs related to Abraham Lincoln.
        ISBN 0-7660-5005-X
        1. Lincoln, Abraham, 1809–1865—Juvenile literature. 2. Presidents—United
States—Biography—Juvenile literature. [1. Lincoln, Abraham, 1809–1865.
2. Presidents] I. Title. II. Series.
E457.905 .A58 2002
973.7'092—dc2 I
[B]
                                                                                    2001004265

Printed in the United States of America

10 9 8 7 6 5 4 3 2 1

To Our Readers: We have done our best to make sure all Internet addresses in this book
were active and appropriate when we went to press. However, the author and the Publisher
have no control over, and assume no liability for, the material available on those Internet
sites or on other Web sites they may link to. The Publisher will try to keep the Report Links
that back up this book up to date on our Web site for three years from the book's
first publication date. Any comments or suggestions can be sent by e-mail to
comments@myreportlinks.com or to the address on the back cover.

Photo Credits: © Corel Corporation, pp. 1 (background), 3, 44; Courtesy of
Abraham Lincoln Historical Digitization Project, p. 18; Courtesy of American
Memory/Library of Congress, pp. 13, 20; Courtesy of Mr. Lincoln's Virtual
Library/Library of Congress, p. 17; Courtesy of MyReportLinks.com Books, p. 4;
Courtesy of the Abraham Lincoln Papers/Library of Congress, p. 39; Courtesy of
the Abraham Lincoln's Research Site, p. 15; Courtesy of Hearts of the Blue &
Gray, p. 23; Courtesy of The History Place presents Abraham Lincoln, pp. 33, 35;
Harper's Weekly, p. 36; Library of Congress, pp. 16, 25; National Archives, pp. 1,
21, 26, 28, 31, 32, 40.

Cover Photos: © Corel Corporation; *Dictionary of American Portraits*, Dover
Publications, Inc., © 1967.

Contents

MyReportLinks.com Books
Great Books, Great Links, Great for Research!

MyReportLinks.com Books present the information you need to learn about your report subject. In addition, they show you where to go on the Internet for more information. The pre-evaluated Report Links, listed on **www.myreportlinks.com**, save hours of research time and link to dozens—even hundreds—of Web sites, source documents, and photos related to your report topic.

To Our Readers:
Each Report Link has been reviewed by our editors, who will work hard to keep only active and appropriate Internet addresses in our books and up to date on our Web site. However, the author and the Publisher have no control over, and assume no liability for, the material available on those Internet sites, or on other Web sites they may link to.

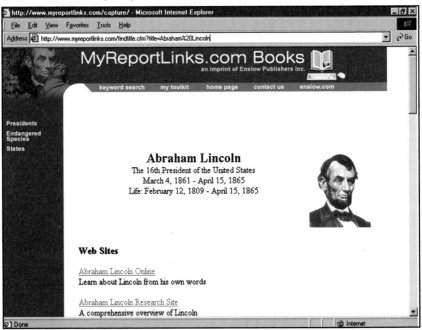

Access:
The Publisher will try to keep the Report Links that back up this book up to date on our Web site for three years from the book's first publication date. Please enter **PLI186K** if asked for a password.

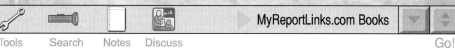
Report Links

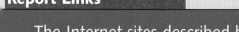

The Internet sites described below can be accessed at
http://www.myreportlinks.com

*EDITOR'S CHOICE

▶ Abraham Lincoln Online
This site is loaded with letters, speeches, and quotes by Lincoln.
You will also find images of the president (photos, prints, stamps,
and sculptures) and a list of Lincoln's successes and failures.

Link to this Internet site from http://www.myreportlinks.com

*EDITOR'S CHOICE

▶ Abraham Lincoln Research Site
One of the most comprehensive sites on Lincoln, covering nearly
every aspect of his life. If you cannot find what you need here,
you will almost certainly find a link to another site that can answer
your questions.

Link to this Internet site from http://www.myreportlinks.com

*EDITOR'S CHOICE

▶ The Emancipation Proclamation
Nearly two years after the start of the Civil War, Lincoln issued the
Emancipation Proclamation, freeing all the slaves in the "rebellious
states." This site has the full text and images of the original document.

Link to this Internet site from http://www.myreportlinks.com

*EDITOR'S CHOICE

▶ The White House: Abraham Lincoln
A useful, concise biography of Lincoln, along with a Fun Fact and
Fast Fact that you may not know. This is good for basic information.

Link to this Internet site from http://www.myreportlinks.com

*EDITOR'S CHOICE

Mr. Lincoln's Virtual Library
The Library of Congress holds a collection of twenty thousand
Abraham Lincoln documents, including drafts of speeches, journal
entries, and correspondence.

Link to this Internet site from http://www.myreportlinks.com

*EDITOR'S CHOICE

The Lincoln Legal Papers
Learn about Lincoln's law practice and his gradual involvement in the
world of politics.

Link to this Internet site from http://www.myreportlinks.com

Report Links

➤ The Internet sites described below can be accessed at
http://www.myreportlinks.com

▶ **Abe Lincoln, Country Lawyer**
Written by biographer Benjamin Thomas, this article tells of Lincoln's life as a lawyer in the late 1840s and early 1850s.

Link to this Internet site from http://www.myreportlinks.com

▶ **Abraham Lincoln Birthplace: National Historic Site**
Enjoy a virtual tour of Lincoln's birthplace, including a rustic cabin like the one in which he was born.

Link to this Internet site from http://www.myreportlinks.com

▶ **Abraham Lincoln Historical Digitization Project**
A wealth of writings by and about Lincoln can be found here. The focus of this site is his time spent living in Illinois.

Link to this Internet site from http://www.myreportlinks.com

▶ **Abraham Lincoln: 16th President of the United States**
All vital statistics of Lincoln's life can be found here in convenient outline form. The site also features some facts about the presidential elections of 1860 and 1864.

Link to this Internet site from http://www.myreportlinks.com

▶ **Assassination of President Lincoln and the Trial of the Assassins**
Brigadier General Henry L. Burnett investigated Lincoln's assassination and served as a prosecutor during the murder trial. This site presents Burnett's memories of this sensational case.

Link to this Internet site from http://www.myreportlinks.com

▶ **Crisis at Fort Sumter**
This site provides a detailed account of the steps leading to the outbreak of war between the North and South.

Link to this Internet site from http://www.myreportlinks.com

Report Links

> The Internet sites described below can be accessed at
> **http://www.myreportlinks.com**

▶**The Dred Scott Case**
This site offers a wealth of information about the 1857 *Dred Scott* case
and the lingering effects of the Supreme Court's decision.

Link to this Internet site from http://www.myreportlinks.com

▶**Ford's Theatre: National Historic Site**
The National Park Service gives a detailed history of Ford's Theatre and
the assassination of President Lincoln.

Link to this Internet site from http://www.myreportlinks.com

▶**Founder's Library: The 19th Century**
Dozens of Lincoln's most memorable speeches, as well as the transcripts
of Lincoln's 1858 debates with Stephen Douglas can be found here.

Link to this Internet site from http://www.myreportlinks.com

➡**The Gettysburg Address**
Included here is the text of the Gettysburg Address, images of drafts
of the speech, and even a rare picture of Lincoln at the Gettysburg
Battlefield.

Link to this Internet site from http://www.myreportlinks.com

Hearts of the Blue & Gray
Cape Girardeau, Missouri, was just one of the hundreds of cities
touched by the Civil War. This site contains descriptions of monuments
to both the Union and Confederacy found in this town. It also contains
an excellent map.

Link to this Internet site from http://www.myreportlinks.com

The History Place Presents Abraham Lincoln
A comprehensive time line of Lincoln's life. The time line begins in
1637 with Englishman Samuel Lincoln's arrival in the United States.

Link to this Internet site from http://www.myreportlinks.com

Report Links

 The Internet sites described below can be accessed at
http://www.myreportlinks.com

▶**Lincoln and the Chicken Bone Case**
This is an account of Lincoln's years as a lawyer. In the Chicken Bone Case, Lincoln represented physicians who were accused of medical errors.

Link to this Internet site from http://www.myreportlinks.com

▶**Lincoln's Greatest Speech?**
Pulitzer Prize-winning author Gary Wills assesses Abraham Lincoln's second inaugural address in this essay. The speech, in Wills's view, was Lincoln's most impressive.

Link to this Internet site from http://www.myreportlinks.com

▶**Lincoln Home: National Historic Site**
The Lincolns lived in this home in Springfield, Illinois, from 1844 until early 1861. You will find photos and details of the history of the house.

Link to this Internet site from http://www.myreportlinks.com

▶**Lincoln Memorial**
This site provides a detailed history of the Lincoln Memorial in Washington, D.C., as well as an extensive biography of Lincoln.

Link to this Internet site from http://www.myreportlinks.com

▶**Lincoln's New Salem**
The historic site of New Salem offers a view of the village as it appeared when Lincoln lived there. This site offers a virtual tour of some of the village's log homes, businesses, and its school.

Link to this Internet site from http://www.myreportlinks.com

▶**Lincoln Wins the Republican Nomination in 1860**
This site offers an account of the behind-the-scenes deal-making that led to the nomination of Lincoln at the 1860 Republican Convention.

Link to this Internet site from http://www.myreportlinks.com

Report Links

The Internet sites described below can be accessed at
http://www.myreportlinks.com

▶**National Archives and Records Administration: Lincoln Assassination Report**
View the District of Columbia police blotter that recorded the attack on Lincoln.

Link to this Internet site from http://www.myreportlinks.com

▶**News of Abraham Lincoln's Death**
Read the *New York Times* coverage of Lincoln's assassination as it appeared in the newspaper on April 16, 1865.

Link to this Internet site from http://www.myreportlinks.com

▶**Portrait of Young Abraham Lincoln**
In 1977, Albert Kaplan purchased an early photograph described as *Portrait of a Young Man*. In time, he became convinced the subject of the photo was a young Abraham Lincoln. This site also features a handful of essays about Lincoln, including a biographical profile.

Link to this Internet site from http://www.myreportlinks.com

▶**Slavery and a House Divided**
Alarmed by the growing gulf between slave and free states, President Lincoln gave his famous "house divided" speech, which is shown here.

Link to this Internet site from http://www.myreportlinks.com

▶**Wet with Blood**
Read more about the shooting of Lincoln and the cloak believed to be worn by Mary Todd Lincoln on the night her husband was assassinated.

Link to this Internet site from http://www.myreportlinks.com

▶**The White House: Mary Todd Lincoln**
This site will provide you with the basic facts about Lincoln's wife, Mary Todd, both before and after their marriage.

Link to this Internet site from http://www.myreportlinks.com

Highlights

1809—*Feb. 12:* Abraham Lincoln is born in a one-room cabin near Hodgenville, Kentucky.

1816—The Lincoln family moves to Indiana.

1818—Abraham's mother, Nancy Hanks Lincoln, dies.

1819—Abraham's father, Thomas Lincoln, marries Sarah Bush Johnston.

1830—The family moves to Illinois.

1831—Lincoln settles in New Salem on his own.

1834—Elected to the Illinois General Assembly; serves four terms.

1836—Earns license to practice law.

1837—Moves to Springfield, Illinois. Works as a circuit-riding lawyer.

1842—Marries Mary Todd.

1846—Elected to the United States House of Representatives.

1856—Helps organize the new Republican Party in Illinois.

1858—Runs for U.S. Senate against Stephen Douglas. Debates Douglas on the expansion of slavery into free territory. Douglas wins Senate seat.

1860—*Nov. 6:* Elected president.

—*Dec.:* South Carolina secedes from the Union, followed quickly by Mississippi, Florida, Alabama, Georgia, Louisiana, and Texas.

1861—*March 4:* First inauguration.

—*April 12:* Confederates fire on Fort Sumter; Civil War begins.

1863—*Jan. 1:* Issues Emancipation Proclamation.

—*Nov. 19:* Delivers Gettysburg Address.

1864—*Nov. 8:* Elected to second term as president.

1865—*March 4:* Second inauguration is held.

—*April 9:* The Civil War ends when General Robert E. Lee surrenders Confederate forces to General Ulysses S. Grant at Appomattox Court House, Virginia.

—*April 14:* Fatally shot by John Wilkes Booth at Ford's Theatre in Washington, D.C.

—*April 15:* Abraham Lincoln dies at fifty-six years of age.

—*April 26:* Booth is shot and killed in a Virginia barn.

—*May 4:* Lincoln is buried with his son William Wallace in Springfield, Illinois.

—*Dec. 6:* Congress ratifies the Thirteenth Amendment; slavery is abolished.

Emancipation, 1863

President Abraham Lincoln sat at his desk in the small White House room he used as an office. Beside him stood his secretary of state, William Seward. Lincoln studied the document that Seward had brought him. In his hand, the president held a gold pen. Slowly, he dipped it into ink and made some scratching marks on a separate piece of paper. Other men wandered in and out of the office as though nothing important was going on.

Lincoln had just come from the White House New Year's reception. He had spent hours shaking the hands of military officers, White House staff, and government officials. The affair had been so tiring that his wife, Mary Todd Lincoln, had to excuse herself. Lincoln's hand was almost numb. He was afraid that his handwriting would be shaky. He did not want anyone to suspect that he had been nervous when he signed this document.

He read the document again:

> That on the first day of January, in the year of our Lord one thousand eight hundred and sixty-three, all persons held as slaves within any State or designated part of a State, the people whereof shall then be in rebellion against the United States, shall be then, thenceforward, and forever free. . . .[1]

At last, he wrote his name in a firm hand. Studying the signature, he said, "There, that will do."[2]

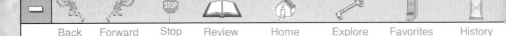
Abraham Lincoln had just signed the Emancipation Proclamation. At this time in history, the Southern states were fighting the Northern states in the Civil War. The South believed it had the right to secede from, or leave, the United States and form its own nation, the Confederate States of America. Southerners also wanted to keep slavery legal in their states, whereas many people in the North wanted to end slavery. As commander-in-chief of the Union Army, Lincoln could declare slavery against the law in rebellious territories. In September 1862, he issued a preliminary emancipation proclamation. During the next few months he carefully rewrote the document many times. The Emancipation Proclamation was officially issued and took effect on January 1, 1863. Unfortunately, his declaration could only be enforced in areas that had been captured by the North. It did not really go far in freeing slaves. Still, the Emancipation Proclamation was tremendously important as a symbolic gesture because it clearly stated Lincoln's position on slavery.

The Union also needed more soldiers, and Lincoln believed that freed slaves would fight in the Union Army. The proclamation reassured Great Britain and France as well. Those countries bought cotton from the Southern states, but they were opposed to slavery. Before the proclamation, the Union government was afraid Britain and France would give their support to the rebels so the cotton trade would continue. Once the proclamation was issued, though, Lincoln knew Britain and France would never fight on the side of the slave states.

Southerners protested the proclamation. Many Northern Republicans, men of Lincoln's own party, argued that they were not fighting a war to free slaves. They were fighting to preserve the Union. On the other side, abolitionists—people who worked to end slavery—thought

Tools   Search   Notes   Discuss   Go!

http://lcweb2.loc.gov/cgi-bin/query/l?presp:1:./temp/~ammem_Xuic::displayType=1:m856sd=cph:m856s - Microsoft Internet ...

File   Edit   View   Favorites   Tools   Help

Address http://lcweb2.loc.gov/cgi-bin/query/l?presp:1:./temp/~ammem_Xuic::displayType=1:m856sd=cph:m856sf=3a05802:@@@pres   Go

Done   Internet

▲ *A painting depicting Lincoln's first reading
of the Emancipation Proclamation.*

the proclamation did not go far enough. They wanted
slavery to be abolished immediately throughout the country.
Lincoln did not have the power to do this, so he appealed to
Congress to pass an amendment to the Constitution
abolishing slavery in the nation.

In January 1865, Congress passed the Thirteenth
Amendment to the Constitution, abolishing slavery as
Lincoln desired. The states did not ratify the amendment
until nine months after his death. He would probably have
been overjoyed. He had taken the first important step
toward ending slavery when he signed the Emancipation
Proclamation on New Year's Day in 1863. He is reported
to have said, "If my name ever goes into history, it will be
for this act."[3]

Chapter 2

Lincoln's Early Life, 1809–1834

Abraham Lincoln was born on February 12, 1809, in a log cabin near what is now called Hodgenville, Kentucky. His parents were Thomas Lincoln and Nancy Hanks Lincoln. They also had a daughter, Sarah, who was born in 1806. After Abe came Thomas, Jr., who was born in 1812 but died as an infant.

Thomas Lincoln was not a successful farmer. His crops did not thrive. In addition, he did not like living in Kentucky, where slavery was commonplace. Although his brothers had owned slaves, Thomas believed it was wrong for one man to own another. In 1816, he moved his family to Indiana, where there was no slavery.

Young Abe sometimes attended school. He probably spent no more than a year in the classroom. The schools he attended were called "blab" schools because they had no books. The students learned by listening to each other recite.

▶ Life with Sally

In 1818, when Abe was nine, his mother died. The following year, his father visited Kentucky and came home with a new wife, Sarah Bush Johnston, who was also called Sally. She brought three children of her own to the marriage—John, Sarah, and Matilda. She was an efficient housekeeper and a good person who loved both Sarah and Abraham Lincoln a great deal. She and Abe were particularly close. She later said that he never gave her a word that was not the absolute truth.[1]

Sarah Johnston encouraged Abe to read. As a young man he read Shakespeare, the Bible, *Aesop's Fables, Robinson Crusoe,* and other classic works. He even read *The Revised Laws of Indiana.* He frequently read at night by the light of the fire.

Abraham worked in the fields with his father. He plowed and planted and was known for his ability to split logs to make rail fences. The nickname "the Rail-splitter," given to him during his political career, refers to this period in his life. Sometimes Abe's father hired him out to

http://home.att.net/~rjnorton/Lincoln81.html - Microsoft Internet Explorer

File　Edit　View　Favorites　Tools　Help

Address http://home.att.net/~rjnorton/Lincoln81.html　Go

ABRAHAM LINCOLN'S PARENTS

Nancy Hanks Lincoln (drawn by Lloyd Ostendorf), Thomas Lincoln, and Sarah Bush Johnston Lincoln

NANCY HANKS LINCOLN, birth mother of Abraham Lincoln, was born on February 5, 1784, in Hampshire County, (West) Virginia. The birth occurred in a cabin along Mike's Run at the foot of New Creek Mountain in what is now Mineral County, West Virginia. Nancy's mother was Lucy Hanks, but nothing is really known about Nancy's father. According to Abraham Lincoln's law partner, William Herndon, Abraham once said that his maternal grandfather was "a well-bred Virginia farmer or planter." During the same conversation, Abraham said of his mother, "God bless my mother; all that I am or ever hope to be I owe to her."

Little is known of Nancy's early life. As a child Nancy was taken by her mother along the Wilderness Road through the

Internet

▲ Abraham's mother, Nancy Hanks Lincoln (left), died when he was very young. His father, Thomas, later married Sarah Bush Johnston (right). She and Lincoln became very close.

work for neighbors. Abe resented this treatment. He was never as close to his father as he was to his stepmother.

Exposure to Slavery

In 1828, a wealthy farmer named Gentry, who lived nearby, wanted to ship his crops and herds to New Orleans for sale. He asked Abe Lincoln to accompany his son on the trip because he knew Lincoln to be trustworthy. On that trip Lincoln saw slaves chained together with only about a foot between them. He said they reminded him of "fish upon a trot-line."[2] He was also shocked when he saw a slave auction.

First Career

Thomas Lincoln moved his family farther west. He took them to a farm near Decatur, Illinois, in 1830, and then deeper into Illinois in 1831. On the second move, when Abraham Lincoln was twenty-two, he decided to get away from farming.[3] He left his family and settled in New Salem, Illinois, where he ran a general store for a man named Denton Offutt.

When Offutt's store failed, Lincoln went into a partnership with William Berry in another store. When Berry died, Abraham Lincoln found himself in debt of more than one thousand dollars from both stores. He eventually repaid the entire debt. His reputation as "Honest Abe" probably came from his time as a

Lincoln as a young man, splitting logs for rail fences.

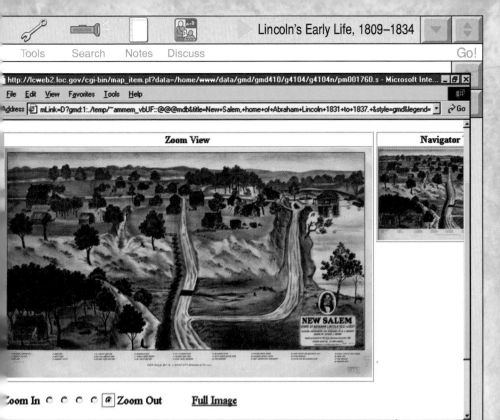

▲ *Lincoln ran a general store in New Salem. This is a map of what the town looked like during Lincoln's time.*

storekeeper. Legend says that he once overcharged a customer by mistake and walked several miles to repay the amount he had overcharged.

Lincoln was also known for his physical strength. Once, when challenged by a man looking for a fight, he showed both his strength and his cleverness. Having bested the other man, he was attacked by the man's friends. Lincoln offered to fight each of them—one at a time. This ended the fight.

Lincoln also told stories to amuse others and to fight depression, which he often suffered from. He was so popular that after both stores failed, the townspeople found work for him as a postmaster and a surveyor.

▶ Military Service

When American Indians and settlers clashed in the Black Hawk War of 1832, Lincoln was named the captain of a rifle company. He was not an efficient military man, and he would sometimes forget the commands to tell his men what he wanted them to do. The company never saw action. At war's end, as the company headed back to New Salem, their horses were stolen. In later years, Lincoln told amusing stories about his military experience—or lack thereof.

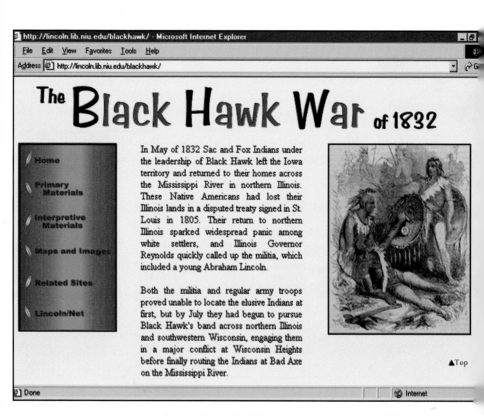

In 1832, Chief Black Hawk led a band of Sac and Fox Indians back to their native Illinois. There, they clashed with the Illinois militia.

Chapter 3

A Growing Political Career, 1834–1861

In 1832, Lincoln's friends persuaded him to run for the Illinois General Assembly, but the Black Hawk War interrupted his campaign and he was defeated. He was beginning to develop political ambitions, however. He started to study law on his own. On his second run, in 1834, Lincoln was elected to the Illinois General Assembly as a member of the Whig Party. Whigs supported high tariffs (taxes on imported goods), internal improvements such as road construction, and a strong central government. Lincoln was reelected in 1836, the same year that he earned his license to practice law. In 1837, he left New Salem to settle in Springfield and became the junior partner in a law firm. He eventually served four terms in the Illinois legislature, supporting himself by traveling through nine counties as a circuit-riding lawyer, trying a wide variety of cases.

▶ Marriage and a New Family

Much has been written about Lincoln's romances, particularly his supposed love for Ann Rutledge, who died very young. It was once believed that they were engaged, but modern study has shown that this was probably not the case. As a young man, Lincoln was apparently self-conscious and ill at ease around women.

In 1839 he met Mary Todd, a wealthy, well-educated young woman from Kentucky. They were engaged, broke the engagement, and then were married rather suddenly on November 4, 1842. Their first year of marriage was

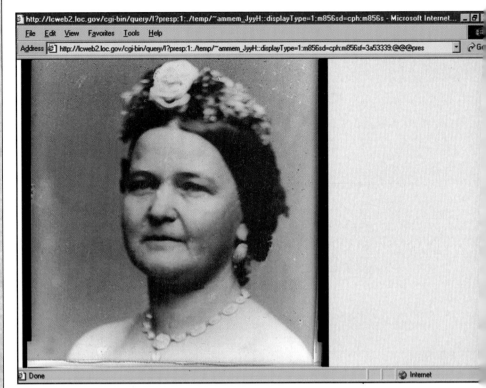

▲ *A photo of Mary Todd Lincoln, taken sometime between 1860 and 1865.*

difficult. Mary was used to having servants, and disliked Lincoln's plain way of life. In addition, he was away much of the time, traveling as a lawyer or attending to legislative business. The two had a genuine affection for each other, in spite of Mary's sometimes hot temper. Lincoln was soon able to buy a comfortable home in Springfield for them.

Abe and Mary Todd Lincoln had four sons: Robert Todd was born in 1843 and was the only son to survive into adulthood; Edwin Baker was born in March 1846 and died in February 1850; William Wallace (Willie) was born in December 1850 and died in February 1862; and Thomas (Tad) was born in 1853 and died in 1871.

U.S. Representative

Lincoln was elected to the U.S. House of Representatives in 1846. He moved his family into a boardinghouse in Washington, D.C., and began his term. The issue of slavery already divided the House. Texas had been admitted to the Union in 1845 as a slave state. Northerners, many of whom opposed slavery, were afraid that if new states decided their own laws on slavery, most would allow it.

When Lincoln entered Congress, the country was at war with Mexico. When the war ended, the United States acquired from Mexico extensive territory in the southwest. Lincoln feared that the new territories would eventually enter the Union as slave states. He hated slavery, but he was willing to put up with it where it already existed in order to preserve the Union. He was, however, completely opposed to expanding slavery.

Lincoln believed that the United States should use its resources to improve roads and build bridges and railroads instead of going to war. He spoke out against President James K. Polk and blamed him for starting the war. This may have cost Lincoln reelection because both President Polk and the Mexican War were popular.

When his term was over, Lincoln returned to Springfield. He was convinced that his national political career was over. Once again, he rode the circuit as a lawyer.

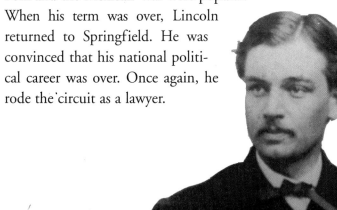

Robert Lincoln

The Missouri Compromise

Slavery was strong in the South, where large plantations needed many field workers to grow cotton. The North had mostly small farms and supported itself with industries such as textile mills, paper plants, furniture factories, and ammunition factories. There was less need for slaves. In addition, some Northerners held religious beliefs against slavery and thought it should be abolished.

When Missouri requested admission to the Union in 1818 as a slave state, Northerners realized that such a plan would give slave states a majority of votes in the legislature. When Maine then applied for statehood as a free state, restoring the balance, Congress admitted Missouri as a slave state but adopted the Missouri Compromise in 1820. The Compromise said that there could be no slavery north of latitude 36°30' (a line running roughly along the southern border of Missouri), except in the state of Missouri.

The Kansas-Nebraska Act

The 1854 passage of the Kansas-Nebraska Act made slavery possible in two states well north of the line drawn by the Missouri Compromise. It also drew Lincoln back into politics. He wrote, "I was losing interest in politics, when the repeal of the Missouri Compromise aroused me again."[1] Congress gave the citizens of Kansas and Nebraska the right to decide if they would be admitted as free or slave states. Thus, the act opened formerly free territories to slavery and cancelled the Missouri Compromise.

Lincoln denounced the Kansas-Nebraska Act and spoke out forcefully against the expansion of slavery. In a day when political speeches were long and full of flowery

Tools   Search   Notes   Discuss   Go!

http://www.rosecity.net/civilwar/capesites/warmap.html - Microsoft Internet Explorer

File   Edit   View   Favorites   Tools   Help

Address http://www.rosecity.net/civilwar/capesites/warmap.html   Go

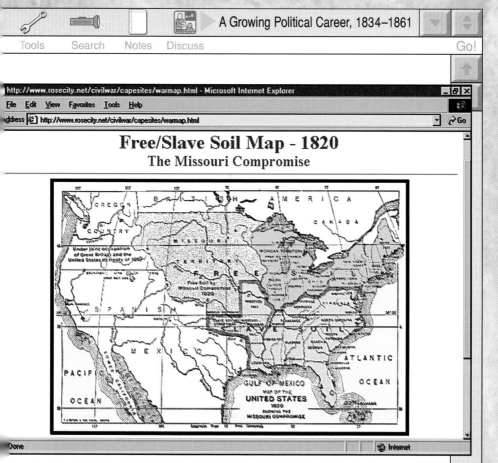

Free/Slave Soil Map - 1820
The Missouri Compromise

Done   Internet

▲ *In 1820, the United States was made up of some states and territories where slavery was legal and some where it was illegal. The Missouri Compromise sought to maintain the balance between slave states and free states.*

language, Lincoln had a distinctive style. He often spoke briefly. He used plain language, and he based his speeches on logic instead of emotion. In 1854, the Whigs had not yet stated their position on slavery. Some Whigs who were strongly opposed to slavery left the party to form the Republican Party. Lincoln attended an 1856 meeting in Bloomington, Illinois, to organize the Free Soil Party in Illinois. In his "lost" speech he spoke without notes against the violence the slavery issue was causing in the United States and of the need to preserve the Union. Journalists in

the audience became so spellbound by his words and his passion that they forgot to write down what he said, or so the story goes. There is no record of the speech. The people at that meeting helped form the Republican Party of Illinois.[2]

Race for the U.S. Senate

In 1858, Illinois Republicans nominated Lincoln for the U.S. Senate. At the convention, he delivered the now-famous speech, "A house divided against itself cannot stand. I believe this government cannot endure, permanently half slave and half free."[3]

Lincoln's opponent for the Senate seat was a longtime acquaintance and bitter political rival, Senator Stephen Douglas of Illinois. Douglas, a Democrat who was seeking reelection, had introduced the Kansas-Nebraska Act in the Senate. He disagreed with Lincoln on the issue of the expansion of slavery. The two men scheduled a series of seven debates in different cities. As a little-known politician, Lincoln probably would not have attracted many listeners. Great crowds came to the debates, however, because Douglas was a prominent national political figure. The debates also made Lincoln known nationally. In those days, members of state legislatures elected U.S. Senators, and the Republicans hoped to gain control of the Illinois legislature in 1858. But, though the Republicans did well in the election, the Democrats retained their majority and picked Douglas, not Lincoln, for the U.S. Senate.

Speaking Out Against Slavery

Lincoln returned to Illinois and his law practice, but he continued to travel and speak against the expansion of slavery. He also believed that there must be no secession

Tools   Search   Notes   Discuss   Go!

RAN AWAY!

FROM THE SUBSCRIBER. My Mulatto Boy, **GEORGE.** Said George is 5 feet 8 inches in height, brown curly Hair, dark coat. I will give **$400** for him alive, and the same sum for satisfactory proof that he has been killed.

Vide **ANTHONY & ELLIS' MAMMOTH** "**UNCLE TOM'S CABIN.**"   **WM. HARRIS.**

▲ Slaves were the property of their masters. They had no freedom and no rights. The issue of slavery divided the nation and split the Union apart in the 1860s.

from the Union. His thinking had been influenced by three things that happened between 1856 and 1860, and by 1859 he was thinking of running for the U.S. presidency.

The first was the decision of the U.S. Supreme Court in the 1857 *Dred Scott* case said that Scott, a slave, could not plead for freedom in a federal court because he was not and never could be a United States citizen. The decision also provided that Congress could not ban slavery from territories not yet admitted to the Union. Secondly, in Kansas, war broke out between proslavery and antislavery groups. The town of Lawrence was burned and dozens of people were killed throughout the state. The state was nicknamed "Bleeding Kansas." Finally, in October 1859 at Harper's Ferry, Virginia, John Brown, a determined abolitionist, seized a federal arsenal and tried to start a slave uprising. Many of Brown's followers were killed. Brown was captured, tried, convicted of treason, and hanged. He became a martyr for the abolitionists' cause.

▶ Republican Presidential Nominee

At the 1860 Republican Party convention in Chicago, Illinois, Lincoln was presented as "Honest Abe, the Rail-splitter." The image of a rail-splitter, someone capable and hard-working, made Lincoln popular in the Midwest, but party members from the East considered him unrefined. They

This cartoon depicts Lincoln being skewered by the bayonets of Southern troops. It shows how much he was disliked and distrusted in the South because of his position on slavery.

expected to nominate William Seward, a prominent antislavery senator from New York. After three ballots, Lincoln was named the Republican presidential nominee.

Candidates for president did not campaign in those days. The members of Lincoln's party campaigned for him. Lincoln societies were formed. They called themselves Wide-Awakes, and they chanted,

> *Old Abe Lincoln came out of the wilderness,*
> *Out of the wilderness,*
> *Out of the wilderness.*
> *Old Abe Lincoln came out of the wilderness,*
> *Down in Illinoy.[4]*

▶ The Price of Victory

Three men ran against Lincoln. The Democratic Party had split in two: the Northern Democrats and the Southern Democrats. Stephen Douglas was the candidate of the Northern Democrats; John Breckinridge, then the vice president, ran for the Southern Democrats. In the West a new party, the Constitutional Unionists, backed former senator John Bell of Tennessee. Lincoln received just under 40 percent of the popular vote and 180 votes in the electoral college—enough to win the presidency. He was elected on November 6, 1860.

Some Southern Democrats believed that a Republican victory meant the end of slavery, but their economy depended on slavery. They said they had no choice but to secede from the Union. They believed they were sovereign states in a voluntary union from which they had every right to withdraw. Between Lincoln's election and inauguration, seven states—South Carolina, Florida, Georgia, Alabama, Mississippi, Louisiana, and Texas—seceded from

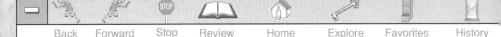
the Union. They joined together as the Confederate States of America. The president leaving office, James Buchanan, blamed the crisis on the Republicans' anti-slavery position. Lincoln watched the Union fall apart and worried about what he, as president, could do to save his country.

In early February 1861, Lincoln gave a brief farewell address to friends in Springfield. Then he and his family boarded a train for Washington, D.C. There had been threats on his life, and bodyguards followed him closely.

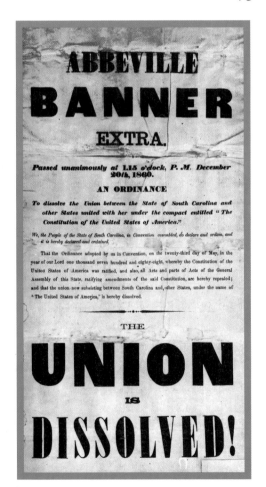

A southern newspaper declares the secession of South Carolina.

Lincoln's First Administration, 1861–1865

In his March 4, 1861 inaugural address, Lincoln swore to uphold the laws of the land, even the Fugitive Slave Law, which he disagreed with. That law held that runaway slaves arrested in the North would be returned to their owners in the South. Lincoln concluded his speech by addressing rebellious Southerners directly with the words, "In your hands, my dissatisfied fellow-countrymen, and not in *mine*, is the momentous issue of civil war. The government will not assail *you*. You can have no conflict without being yourselves the aggressors."[1]

▶ Civil War

One of the first problems Lincoln faced as president concerned getting supplies to federal seaports in the South. If Lincoln withdrew troops from these seaports, he would be effectively recognizing the government of the seceded states. If he sent supplies, he risked war. Lincoln sent supplies. A fleet with food and other goods approached Fort Sumter in South Carolina on April 12. Confederate forces fired on the fort, signaling the start of the Civil War. They allowed the fleet to evacuate Major Robert Anderson and his men from the fort. As Lincoln had said in his inaugural address, Southerners had begun the conflict. Now Lincoln could defend the Union.

Congress did not convene until July. In the meantime, Lincoln ordered Southern ports blockaded to cut off

supplies to Confederate forces. He called for 75,000 volunteers for the army. He suspended the writ of Habeas Corpus—laws that protect citizens against unlawful arrest—in areas where there were known to be Southern sympathizers. He clearly demonstrated that he intended to keep tight control of national affairs.

Two days after Fort Sumter was fired on, Virginia seceded from the Union. North Carolina, Tennessee, and Arkansas followed quickly. The Confederacy numbered eleven states. Confederate troops almost surrounded Washington, D.C. Standing at White House windows, Lincoln could see their campfires in Virginia, less than thirty miles away. The White House was barricaded. Armed men slept outside the president's bedroom.

▶ A Call to Arms

The United States at that time had only a small and disorganized army, no draft (mandatory military service), and few officers with military training. When Lincoln called for volunteers, many towns raised their own volunteer regiments. Later in the war, conscription (or draft laws) would cause major riots in the North, and several men were killed. Men resented being forced to leave their jobs and families to fight, especially if they thought they were fighting to free the slaves. The South, by contrast, had a strong military tradition. Most of the nation's military schools were there. Recognizing his own lack of military knowledge, Lincoln studied books on military strategy and tactics.

Soon after Lincoln's call for volunteers, there were ten thousand soldiers in Washington, D.C. People began to believe the war would be short. They thought one battle would win it. Lincoln ordered General Irvin McDowell to

▲ When the Civil War began in 1861, the White House and the president had to be guarded by the Northern Army.

march his troops toward Richmond, Virginia, the Confederate capital. McDowell delayed for a week, long enough for Southern spies to learn of his plans and send troops to meet him. The two armies met July 21, 1861 at the First Battle of Bull Run (Confederates called it Manassas) in northern Virginia. Citizens from Washington, D.C., packed picnic baskets and rode to the battle site in carriages to watch a quick victory. The Union seemed to be winning most of the day, but late in the afternoon General McDowell sent word to Lincoln that the battle was lost. He was retreating. There was panic on the battlefield as frightened spectators tried to beat

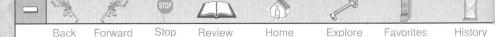
the retreating soldiers to the safety of the nation's capital. The Union suffered 3,000 casualties (which included those soldiers who were killed, wounded, captured, or missing) at Bull Run that day; the Confederacy lost 2,000. Lincoln knew it would be a long war.

Lincoln appointed General George B. McClellan to be "Commander of the Army and Department of the Potomac" and then commander of the entire Union Army in 1861. His soldiers adored "Little Mac," as they called him. He trained them tirelessly, paraded endlessly, and promised glorious victories. But McClellan did not fight.

Lincoln faced other problems. In Missouri, without Lincoln's permission, General John C. Frémont issued an emancipation proclamation freeing all slaves whose owners supported the Confederacy. Lincoln modified Frémont's proclamation because he feared it would anger the border states that remained in the Union. He dismissed Frémont. The same year, an ambitious navy captain stopped a British packet ship, the *Trent*, on the high seas and removed two Confederate ambassadors. Great Britain threatened war if the prisoners were not released. Lincoln turned the men over to the British.

▶ Trouble at Home

Lincoln's family life was also difficult. No matter what his wife did in Washington, Mary Todd Lincoln was criticized. People said she was unrefined, wore bright colors and low-cut necklines, and spent too much to refurbish the shabby White House. Then, in February 1862, the Lincolns' son Willie died at the age of twelve. Both parents were

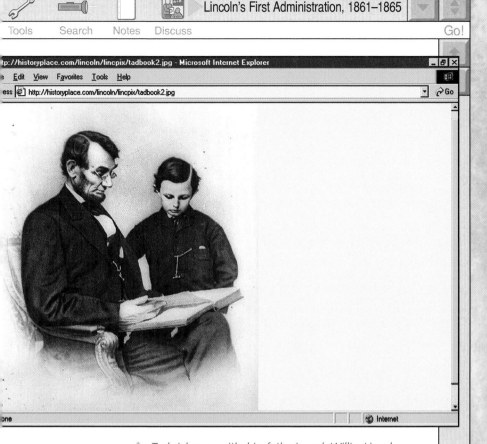

tp://historyplace.com/lincoln/lincpix/tadbook2.jpg - Microsoft Internet Explorer

Edit View Favorites Tools Help

ess http://historyplace.com/lincoln/lincpix/tadbook2.jpg

Tad (above, with his father) and Willie Lincoln (at far left) were well loved by their parents. Sadly, neither boy lived to adulthood.

devastated, but Mrs. Lincoln was too upset to attend his funeral. She was criticized for grieving too hard and too long. Later there were false rumors that she was a spy because several members of her family fought for the Confederacy.

Lincoln was also criticized: for fighting a war to free the slaves, for not working hard enough to free the slaves, for not winning the war, for ignoring Congress, and for listening to citizens. Lincoln knew that military victory without the support of the country would be meaningless. Each day citizens paraded through his office. Some came to thank him, some brought gifts, some wanted to shake

his hand. The president prized these sessions. He made countless civil service appointments, always supporting the Republican Party. He was particularly known for pardoning deserting soldiers, against the wishes of his generals. He understood what he called "legs" cases, where "it was not the soldier who had deserted in battle, but his legs which had got the better of him."[2]

Other Presidential Work

During the war, Lincoln helped institute several important nonmilitary policies. He pushed the Homestead Act through Congress. This act granted 160 acres in the West to any citizen who would improve the land and could prove that he or she had lived on it for five years. This opened land in the West for settlement. It also pointed toward the admission of more free states to the Union. Lincoln signed the Internal Revenue Act, which gave the government power to collect taxes to pay for the war. The National Banking Act put banks under federal, rather than state control, and established a uniform currency. Lincoln also established the Department of Agriculture and greatly increased railroad construction. He provided for land-grant colleges, where federal support would make education available to many more citizens.

Union Army in Trouble

The war, however, consumed much of Lincoln's time and energy. General Ulysses S. Grant, an almost unknown soldier, was winning victories at Shiloh and Memphis in Tennessee and at Corinth in Mississippi. General McClellan, however, continued to disappoint Lincoln.

McClellan laid siege to Richmond, Virginia, the Confederate capital. The accepted strategy of the day was

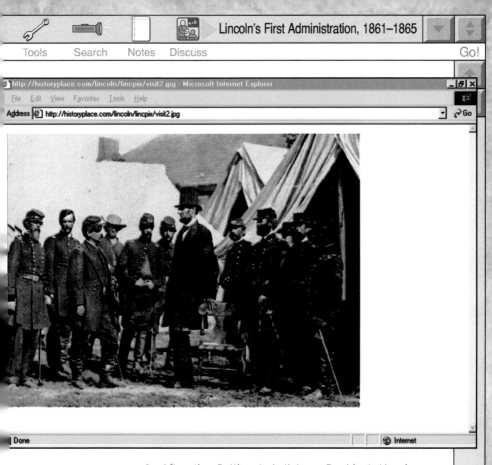

http://historyplace.com/lincoln/lincpix/visit2.jpg - Microsoft Internet Explorer

File Edit View Favorites Tools Help

Address http://historyplace.com/lincoln/lincpix/visit2.jpg

Done | Internet

▲ *After the Battle at Antietam, President Lincoln visited General McClellan at the battlefield. Soon after, Lincoln replaced McClellan with General Ambrose Burnside.*

to capture enemy cities. Soldiers argued that when enough cities had been captured, the enemy would give up. Lincoln felt, however, that Union forces must conquer the rebel army, not just capture its cities. Outside Richmond, McClellan stalled. Lincoln begged him to attack, but McClellan waited for more men, more horses. Confederate forces finally attacked and drove the Union forces away from Richmond. At Antietam, Maryland, in September 1862, the Confederate Army was forced to retreat but the Union Army did not pursue them. Lincoln was dismayed that the Confederates retreated unchallenged. He replaced

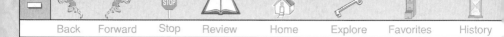
McClellan with General Ambrose Burnside in November 1862, but he also performed poorly. Burnside was replaced by General Joseph Hooker, who lost the Battle of Chancellorsville. Lincoln replaced Hooker with General George Meade, who also let the Confederates withdraw.

Defeat followed defeat. Although they ultimately won the battle, General Grant's troops suffered great losses at Shiloh in April 1862. The Union lost several important battles in Virginia: the Second Battle of Bull Run in August 1862, Fredericksburg in November 1862, and Chancellorsville in May 1863 (17,000 men were lost in this battle alone).

▶ Gettysburg

The Battle of Gettysburg, Pennsylvania, took place on July 1 through 3, 1863. It was the first major Union victory and one of the few battles fought on Union soil. It marked a turning point in the war. General Meade again concentrated on driving the invaders away and did not attack. Lincoln later made Grant chief of all federal armies.

Four months after the Battle of Gettysburg, Lincoln was asked to speak at the dedication of a national cemetery at the battlefield. As he rode to the ceremony, he completed his address. The main speaker, Edward Everett, spoke for over two hours. Lincoln followed him and spoke for about three minutes. He delivered the Gettysburg Address. Lincoln thought the speech was a failure. Today it is a classic of American rhetoric, from its "four score and seven years ago" beginning, to the famous "that government of the people, by the people, and for the people, shall not perish from the earth" ending.

The Election of 1864

The 1864 election was a low point for Lincoln. He was at war with Congress over Reconstruction procedures. Reconstruction was to be the plan for bringing the rebel states back into the Union. His own party insulted him by nearly replacing him with another candidate. Some said he was bloodthirsty. Others said he was too generous with the Confederacy. He had not yet won the war. He was convinced that he would not win the general election. Then, General William Tecumseh Sherman marched through Georgia, capturing Atlanta for the Union Army. His victories helped gain support for Lincoln. The Democrats nominated General George McClellan. Because the Confederacy was now falling apart, Lincoln carried all but three states to win the election.

An End in Sight

By autumn 1864, the South's manpower and resources were becoming exhausted. It was clear that the North would win the war. Lincoln became preoccupied with Reconstruction—the process of reuniting North and South under one government. He also worried about what to do with the freed slaves. He recognized that they would not be able to govern themselves or even provide for themselves immediately. This would be a burden to the country.

Lincoln wanted a plan that would bring the rebellious states back into the Union as easily as possible. In December 1864 he issued the Proclamation of Amnesty and Reconstruction. If 10 percent of the citizens of a Confederate state would take an oath of allegiance to the Union, that state could apply for readmission. The plan was not popular with many Northern politicians.

Chapter 5

The Assassination, 1865

Lincoln's second term as president was brief. In his Second Inaugural Address on March 4, 1865, he used the now-famous phrase, "With malice toward none; with charity for all." Those words defined his formula for Reconstruction.

By early April, Richmond, Virginia, had been taken. Jefferson Davis, president of the Confederacy, escaped. General Robert E. Lee, commander of the Confederate forces, was on the run in Virginia. When Grant surrounded his troops, Lee surrendered at Appomattox Court House, Virginia, on April 9, 1865.

In Washington, there was wild celebration. People covered the White House lawn. Lincoln appeared at a window and asked the band to play "Dixie," calling it one of the best tunes he knew. Then he asked for "The Star-Spangled Banner" and "Battle Hymn of the Republic."

▶ A Tragic End

On Friday, April 14, the Lincolns went for a carriage ride. Mary commented that Abe seemed cheerful. He told her, "We must both be more cheerful in the future; between the war and the loss of our darling Willie, we have been very miserable."[1] He talked of traveling together when his second term was over and of practicing law again.[2]

The Lincolns were supposed to see a play that night called *Our American Cousin* at Ford's Theater in Washington, D.C. Both of them were tired, however, and considered staying home. The president decided some relaxation would do them good. Apparently the guard assigned to protect the president either fell asleep or left his post to get a better view of the play. John Wilkes Booth, an actor and a Southerner bitterly upset at the loss of the war, stepped into Lincoln's box and shot the president once in the back of the head. Then Booth leaped over the railing onto the stage, breaking his leg in the fall. He escaped, but he was shot and killed twelve days later.

Lincoln, still alive, was carried to a boardinghouse across the street. He died early the next morning. He was

On the night of April 14, 1865, Abraham and Mary Lincoln went to see a play at Ford's Theatre. There, John Wilkes Booth, angry that the South had lost the war, shot President Lincoln in the back of the head.

PRESIDENT LINCOLN'S FUNERAL PROCESSION IN WASHINGTON CITY.—[See Page 253.]

▲ Many people gathered to catch a glimpse of Lincoln's funeral procession as it traveled through the streets of Washington, D.C.

the first American president to be assassinated. Mary Todd Lincoln was too upset to do more than request that the president be buried in Springfield, Illinois.

▶ A Grieving Nation

Private services were held in the East Room of the White House. Then, the funeral procession brought Lincoln's coffin to the Rotunda of the Capitol Building. Mourners stood in a line stretching more than a mile, waiting hours for a turn to file past the coffin.

Telegraph communication was newly available to carry the news instantly throughout the country. Even those who had criticized Lincoln grieved. Songs were written

Tools   Search   Notes   Discuss   Go!

with such titles as "We Mourn Our Country's Loss" and "Farewell, Father, Guardian, and Friend." On April 21, a train carrying Lincoln's body and that of his young son Willie left Washington. Willie's body had been removed from a Washington grave so he could be reburied next to his father. People lined the tracks, silent in their grief. Bonfires were lit along the way. The train stopped in eleven cities. In each, the coffin was unloaded and placed on a bier (a stand) so that people could say their goodbyes. Lincoln and Willie were buried together in Springfield in early May 1865.

Chapter 6 ▶

Lincoln's Legacy

Abraham Lincoln's place in history as one of the United States' most important and admired presidents is secure. He led the nation through the Civil War; the most disruptive event in national history. With friends and enemies alike, he was patient, kind, and just. His devotion to his country and its Constitution never wavered. He presided over "a new birth of freedom," as he called it in the Emancipation Proclamation—a United States in which blacks as well as whites were free. "Mr. Lincoln was not only a great President," said Frederick Douglass, the African-American abolitionist leader, "but a *great man*— too great to be small in anything. In his company I was never in any way reminded of my humble origin, or of my unpopular color."[1]

Lincoln's career also illustrated the American dream that anyone, rich or poor, well educated or self-taught, can achieve success. The story of Lincoln learning to read by the fire in a log cabin and eventually becoming president of the United States is treasured as a national legend.

Lincoln was also one of our most eloquent presidents. He left the nation a legacy of speeches and phrases that ring in our ears to this day. Students often memorize the entire Gettysburg Address, and almost everyone recognizes the ringing opening, "Four score and seven years ago, our forefathers brought forth. . . ." Other phrases are equally memorable: "With malice toward none; with charity for all;" "A house divided against itself cannot stand."

Lincoln also had a strong sense of humor. His ability to see the absurd in everyday events helped carry him through the dark days of the Civil War. Several Lincoln joke books were popular in the North, such as *Old Abe's Jokes* or *Wit at the White House*.

▶ Remembered in Art and Song

Lincoln's legacy includes images familiar to every American. We see his face on the tiny copper penny and the massive granite statue of the Lincoln Memorial in Washington. Some of the most dramatic photographs of Lincoln were taken by Mathew Brady, a Civil War photographer. Brady captured Lincoln's deep sadness during the war. Because of hundreds of portraits and statues, the name "Abraham Lincoln" brings to every mind's eye a tall, lanky figure dressed in black. A stovepipe hat sat atop his head, his chin hidden by a beard, his eyes dark and often sad.

The Library of Congress houses a collection entitled *We'll Sing to Abe Our Song*. It contains sheet music written to and about the sixteenth president from his 1859 campaign to the symphony composed on the one hundredth anniversary of his death.[2]

Lincoln is also the subject of countless biographies and numerous poems. Walt Whitman, an American poet who lived and wrote through Lincoln's presidency and most of the nineteenth century, paid tribute to Lincoln in several poems. "When Lilacs Last in the Dooryard Bloom'd" and "O Captain! My Captain!" are Whitman's most famous elegies to Lincoln. The short poem "This Dust Was Once the Man" is less well known, but it is a powerful tribute to Abraham Lincoln, the Great Emancipator.

This Dust Was Once the Man

This dust was once the man,
Gentle, plain, just, and resolute, under whose
*   cautious hand,*
Against the foulest crime in history in any land
*   or age,*
Was saved the Union of these states.[3]

▲ The Lincoln Memorial in Washington, D.C., pays
tribute to this great leader.

Chapter Notes

Chapter 1. Emancipation, 1863

1. Abraham Lincoln, *Speeches and Writings, 1859–1865* (New York: Library of America, 1989), p. 424.

2. Stephen B. Oates, *With Malice Toward None: The Life of Abraham Lincoln* (New York: Harper & Row, 1977), p. 333.

3. Ibid.

Chapter 2. Lincoln's Early Life, 1809–1834

1. Maxim E. Armbruster, *The Presidents of the United States and Their Administrations from Washington to Reagan* (New York: Horizon Press, 1982), p. 174.

2. Bruce Chadwick, *The Two American Presidents: A Dual Biography of Abraham Lincoln and Jefferson Davis* (Secaucus, N.J.: Carol Publishing Group, 1999), p. 25.

3. Stephen B. Oates, *With Malice Toward None: The Life of Abraham Lincoln* (New York: Harper & Row, 1977), p. 10.

Chapter 3. A Growing Political Career, 1834–1861

1. Abraham Lincoln, *The Collected Works of Abraham Lincoln*, Roy P. Basler, ed. (New Brunswick, N.J.: Rutgers University Press, 1953), vol. III, p. 512.

2. Bruce Chadwick, *The Two American Presidents: A Dual Biography of Abraham Lincoln and Jefferson Davis* (Secaucus, N.J.: Carol Publishing Group, 1999), pp. 74–75.

3. Abraham Lincoln, *The Collected Works of Abraham Lincoln*, Roy P. Basler, ed. (New Brunswick, N.J.: Rutgers University Press, 1953), vol. II, p. 461.

4. James Daugherty, *Abraham Lincoln* (New York: The Viking Press, 1968), p. 100.

Chapter 4. Lincoln's First Administration, 1861–1865

1. Abraham Lincoln, *The Collected Works of Abraham Lincoln*, Roy P. Basler, ed. (New Brunswick, N.J.: Rutgers University Press, 1953), vol. IV, p. 271.

2. H. G. Pitt, *Abraham Lincoln* (Phoenix Mill, Great Britain: Sutton Publishing Ltd., 1998), p. 60.

Chapter 5. The Assassination, 1865

1. Stephen B. Oates, *With Malice Toward None: The Life of Abraham Lincoln* (New York: Harper & Row, 1977), p. 429.

2. Ibid.

Chapter 6. Lincoln's Legacy

1. Frederick Douglass, *Life and Times of Frederick Douglass* (New York: Collier Books, 1962), pp. 365–366.

2. Library of Congress, Rare Book and Special Collections Division, Alfred Whital Stern Collection of Lincolniana, *"We'll Sing to Abe Our Song": Sheet Music about Lincoln, Emancipation, and the Civil War,* <http://lcweb2.loc.gov/ammem/scsmhtml/ scsmhome.html> (November 6, 2000).

3. Walt Whitman, "This Dust Was Once the Man," from *Leaves of Grass,* <http://www2.cddc.vt.edu/gutenberg/etext98/lvgrs10.txt> (November 6, 2000).

Further Reading

Burchard, Peter. *Lincoln & Slavery.* New York: Simon & Schuster Children's Publishing, 1999.

Burns, Kenneth. *Civil War.* New York: Alfred A. Knopf, Inc., 1999.

Freedman, Russell. *Lincoln: A Photobiography.* Boston: Houghton Mifflin, 1987.

Graves, Kerry A. *The Civil War.* Mankato, Minn.: Capstone Press, Inc., 2001.

Holzer, Harold, ed. *Abraham Lincoln the Writer: A Treasury of His Greatest Speeches and Letters.* Honesdale, Pa.: Boyd's Mills Press, 2000.

Judson, Karen. *Abraham Lincoln.* Springfield, N.J.: Enslow Publishers, Inc., 1998.

Marrin, Albert. *Commander in Chief: Abraham Lincoln and the Civil War.* New York: New American Library, 1997.

Murphy, Jim. *The Long Road to Gettysburg.* Boston: Houghton Mifflin, 1992.

Sandburg, Carl. *Abe Lincoln Grows Up.* New York: Harcourt, Brace and Company, 1975.

Somerlott, Robert. *The Lincoln Assassination in American History.* Springfield, N.J.: Enslow Publishers, Inc., 1998.

Streissguth, Thomas, ed. *The Civil War: The South.* San Diego, Calif.: Greenhaven Press, Inc., 2001.

Sullivan, George E. *Abraham Lincoln.* New York: Scholastic, Inc., 2001.

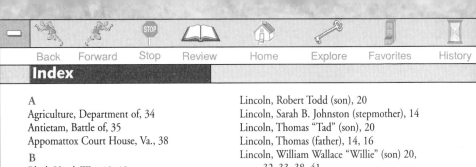